WE COME FROM

Japan

TERESA FISHER

WAYLAND

WE COME FROM

Brazil • China • France
Germany • India • Jamaica • Japan
Kenya • Nigeria • South Africa

The people you are about to meet live in Tokyo, the capital city of Japan.
Like any country, Japan has many different types of lifestyle. People
live in the countryside as well as in towns and cities.

Cover: Eriko, her brother Takahiro and some friends.

Title page: From top to bottom: Takahiro gets ready to throw a
baseball; skyscrapers tower over Tokyo; the Fujii family scours the
beach at Izu for shells; two girls walk to school; and a man attempts
to go parascending.

Contents page: A group of children play in an inner-city park.

Index: Eriko and her dad look out to sea through a telescope.

**All Wayland books encourage
children to read and help them improve their literacy.**

✓ The contents page, page numbers, headings and index
help locate specific pieces of information.

✓ The glossary reinforces alphabetic knowledge and
extends vocabulary.

✓ The further information section suggests other books
dealing with the same subject.

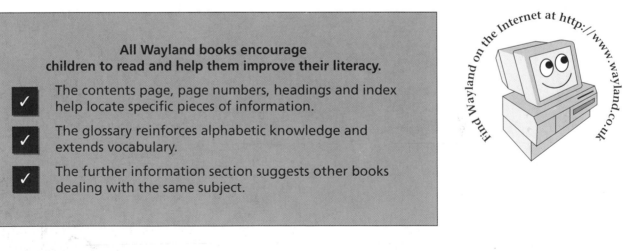

find Wayland on the Internet at http://www.wayland.co.uk

Series editor: Katie Orchard
Designer: Jean Wheeler
Production controller: Tracy Fewtrell

Picture Acknowledgements: All the photographs in
this book were taken by Steve Benbow, except for
Jim Holmes 19, 21, 29 (top left and bottom right);
and Teresa Fisher 29 (centre right). The map
artwork on page 4 is produced by Peter Bull.

First published in 1999 by Wayland Publishers
Limited
61 Western Road, Hove
East Sussex, BN3 1JD, England

© Copyright 1999 Wayland Publishers Limited

British Library Cataloguing in Publication Data
Fisher, Teresa
   We come from Japan
   1. Japan - Geography - Juvenile literature
   2. Japan - Social conditions - 1945- - Juvenile
   literature
   I. Title II. Japan
   952'.049

ISBN 0 7502 2225 5

Typeset by Jean Wheeler, England

Printed and bound by G. Canale & C. S.p.A., Turin

Contents

Welcome to Japan

'My name is Eriko. I am standing with my family in front of our house.' Eriko.

Eriko is eight years old. She lives with her parents, her brother Takahiro and her sister Kumiko. Their home is in Tokyo, the capital city of Japan. You can see where it is on the map on page five.

▲ *From left to right:*
Kumiko
Takako (Eriko's mum)
Takahiro
Hediki (Eriko's dad)
Eriko

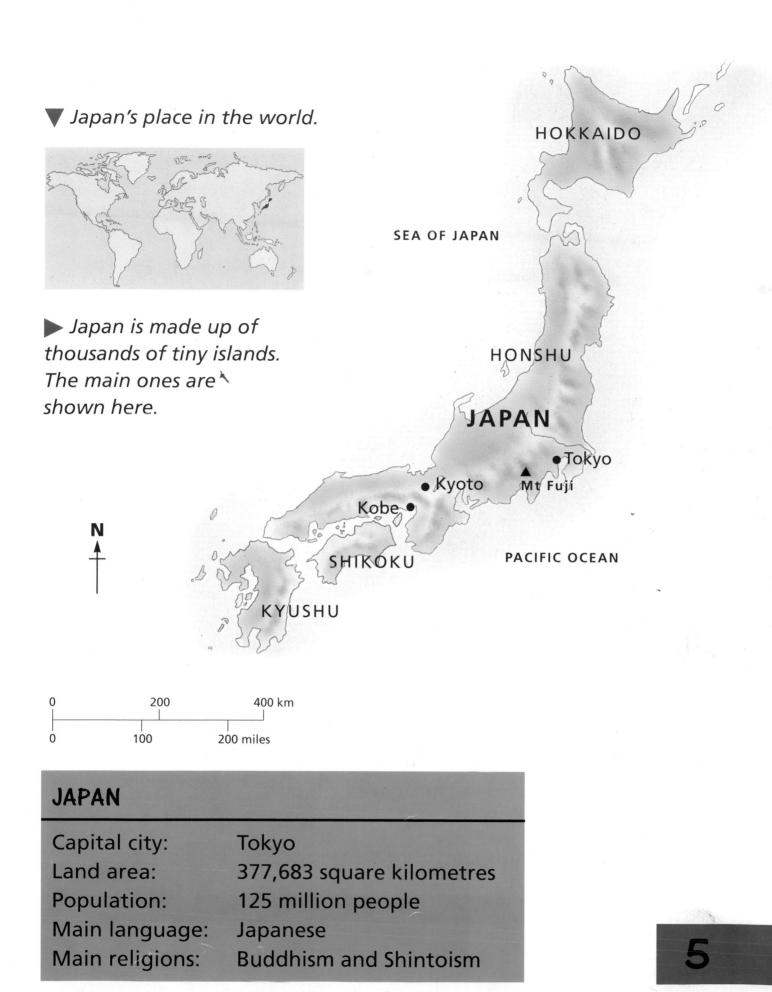

▼ *Japan's place in the world.*

▶ *Japan is made up of thousands of tiny islands. The main ones are shown here.*

HOKKAIDO

SEA OF JAPAN

HONSHU

JAPAN

● Tokyo

● Kyoto
▲ Mt Fuji

Kobe ●

N

SHIKOKU

PACIFIC OCEAN

KYUSHU

0	200	400 km
0	100	200 miles

JAPAN

Capital city:	Tokyo
Land area:	377,683 square kilometres
Population:	125 million people
Main language:	Japanese
Main religions:	Buddhism and Shintoism

The Land and Weather

Japan is a long, narrow country made up of 3,922 islands. Most Japanese live on just four islands – Hokkaido, Shikoku, Kyushu and the main island, Honshu. Japan's nearest neighbours are Russia, Korea and China.

▲ Japan's capital city, Tokyo, has a population of 13 million people.

Three-quarters of Japan is covered with hills and mountains. There are many volcanoes. Some of them let off gases that smell just like rotten eggs.

▲ *Japan's tallest mountain is a dormant volcano called Mount Fuji.*

'In the summer I visit the beach with my family to get away from the busy city.' Eriko.

Japan has very little flat land for farming. Hilly land is always terraced and rice is the main crop.

Winter is cold and snowy and summer is hot. Autumn brings typhoons. Japan also suffers from earthquakes, and schools have regular earthquake safety drills.

▲ *Tall skyscrapers have been built to make the most of small areas of flat land.*

▶ *Rice is grown in flooded fields called paddies.*

◀ *Fishing boats in a harbour. The Japanese catch more fish than any other people in the world.*

9

At Home

Most Japanese people live in flats, in the large cities along the coast of Honshu island. The land here is flat enough to build on. Japanese cities are very crowded, especially Tokyo, where Eriko lives.

▲ *Apartment buildings jostle for space in Tokyo.*

◄ *Eriko's family has a balcony to hang the washing on.*

▶ *The people who live in this block of flats have a park nearby.*

11

Eriko's house is small, but it has everything that the family needs. Eriko sleeps in the same room as her parents. They sleep on thin mattresses called *futons*, which they keep in a cupboard during the day and roll out at night.

'We have all the latest technology at home. I'm playing my favourite video game.' Eriko.

▶ *Eriko's mum has everything she needs in her small kitchen.*

Some Japanese people live in traditional-style homes. These have small rooms, and doors made of paper. They have very little furniture and *tatami* mats on the floor.

▼ *This woman lives in a traditional Japanese home.*

Japanese Food

Breakfast, lunch and dinner in Japan usually include boiled rice, fish and cooked, raw or pickled vegetables. More unusual dishes include pufferfish, which can be poisonous if not cooked properly, or grasshopper, which is sometimes eaten as a snack.

▼ *The Japanese often eat fish raw, in dishes such as* sashimi.

The Japanese are always very polite. Before eating a meal, they always say *'itadakimasu'* which means 'I gratefully accept my meal'.

▶ *There are always lots of foods to choose from in the supermarkets.*

▼ *People sometimes stop at street stalls to buy a tasty snack.*

15

Eriko's family eat their food with chopsticks, instead of knives and forks. Eriko finds some foods, such as rice, difficult to pick up with chopsticks. Sometimes she has to lift the bowl up to her mouth so that she doesn't make a mess.

'Mum thinks it's funny when I can't pick up my noodles using chopsticks!' Eriko.

◄ *Eriko's mum tries some fresh fish at the local fish shop.*

Eriko's mum, like all good Japanese cooks, takes great care to make the food look nice. She likes to choose bowls that are the correct colour, shape and size so that the meal looks really tasty.

▼ *There are always lots of different dishes for dinner at Eriko's house.*

At Work

Japan is famous for making electronic goods, such as computers, stereos and videos. A lot of people in Japan's car industry, too. Eriko's dad owns a shop that sells umbrellas. He works very hard, and often keeps the shop open quite late.

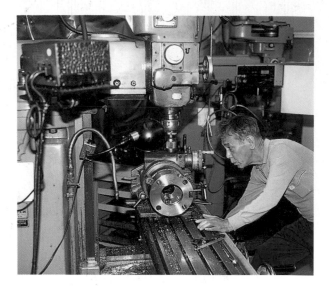

▲ *Factories provide jobs for many Japanese workers.*

▶ *This woman is harvesting some apples. Until recently, only men worked in Japan.*

'I like working here – we are very busy, especially when it's raining!' Eriko's dad.

19

At School

In Japan, all children go to school from the age of six. Japanese schools are very strict. Eriko is learning history, art, geography, mathematics and games. She also has lessons in Japanese language, which she finds difficult.

'Mum takes me to school on her bicycle every morning.' Eriko.

▼ *Most Japanese classes have about 30 children.*

▶ *This girl is learning how to write the Japanese alphabet.*

21

▶ *Takahiro often has to read aloud in front of his class.*

Eriko's brother, Takahiro, goes to the local junior high school. Takahiro wants to do well in his exams. He has extra lessons after school to help him pass.

'Eriko's lucky because she doesn't have to do as much homework as me.' Takahiro.

Schoolchildren have to work hard so that they can go to university when they are eighteen. Many even spend their holidays having extra lessons. When he's not working, Takahiro likes to play volleyball, or go skateboarding.

▼ *These students are playing volleyball in their P.E. lesson.*

Spare Time

The Japanese love to play sports in their spare time. Baseball, golf and martial arts, such as judo and karate, are especially popular. Sumo wrestling always gets a big audience. Eriko likes to have fun in-line skating with her friends.

▲ *These people are about to go boating.*

▶ *Takahiro is mad about skateboarding.*

24

'I got my in-line skates for my birthday. I like to use them every day!' Eriko.

Looking Ahead

Japan is a very modern country, where every home has the latest technology. But it is also a country with ancient traditions. Older Japanese people are worried that these traditions may begin to disappear in the future.

▲ *Many Japanese families mix modern technology with traditional lifestyles.*

'I want to have a job working with computers when I'm older.' Eriko.

▶ *At night, the lights of Japan's modern capital city shine brightly.*

27

Jan, Ken, Pon!

Jan, Ken, Pon (stone, scissors and paper) is one of the first games that Japanese children learn.

- The game is played with two people. Both players make a fist with one hand.

- They then both gently tap their fists on the table at the same time, three times.

- On the third time, they show paper (a flat hand), stone (a fist) or scissors (two fingers open to look like scissors).

▲ *Takahiro plays* Jan, Ken, Pon *with his dad. Paper beats stone ...*

- The scoring is easy. Paper wraps stone, scissors cut paper, stone breaks scissors.

- The player to win each round gets one point. If both players make the same sign, they can have another turn.

- The player with the most points wins the game.

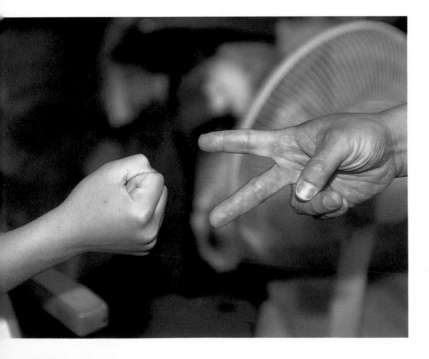

◀ *... stone beats scissors!*

Japan Fact File

Money Facts

◄ Japan's money is the yen, written ¥. There are notes for 1,000, 5,000 and 10,000 yen and coins for 1, 5, 10, 50, 100 and 500 yen. £1 is worth about 230 yen.

Difficult Language

The Japanese language is one of the most complicated languages in the world. It is very difficult to read and write. In school, children learn to write using special ink, paper and brushes.

The Japanese Flag

◄ The Japanese flag is a red circle, to represent the sun, on a white background. Japan is often nicknamed 'Land of the rising sun'.

Ruler

There is no king or queen in Japan. The country is ruled by an Emperor who lives in Tokyo.

National Anthem

The Japanese national anthem is called *Kimigayo*, which means 'His Majesty's Reign'. The words come from a poem which is over 1,000 years old. Singers wish the Emperor a happy reign of 10,000 years!

Mountain Facts

► The highest point in Japan is Mount Fuji (3,776 metres). Most Japanese people try to climb it once in their lifetime.

Water Facts

The longest river is River Tone (322 kilometres) and the largest lake is Lake Biwa (673 square kilometres).

Traditional Costume

◄ Japanese traditional dress is a *kimono* and wooden slippers called *geta*. This is worn by men and women for special occasions including weddings and religious festivals. Some women paint their faces white and wear bright red lipstick. Ladies trained in traditional singing and dancing are called *geisha* girls.

Fast Trains

▼ *Shinkansen,* or 'bullet trains', travel at up to 250 km per hour and are never late.

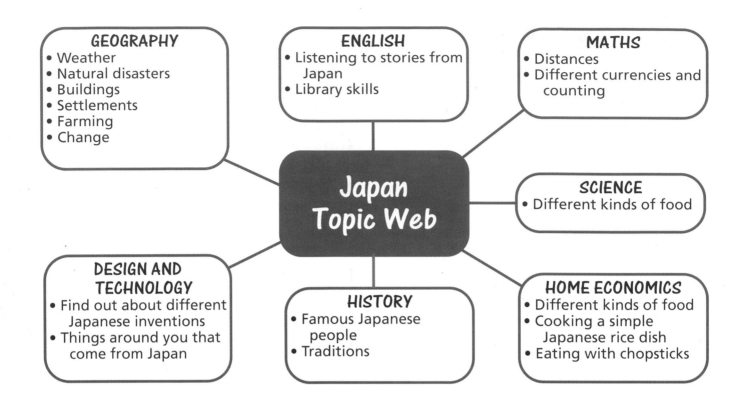

GEOGRAPHY
- Weather
- Natural disasters
- Buildings
- Settlements
- Farming
- Change

ENGLISH
- Listening to stories from Japan
- Library skills

MATHS
- Distances
- Different currencies and counting

Japan Topic Web

SCIENCE
- Different kinds of food

DESIGN AND TECHNOLOGY
- Find out about different Japanese inventions
- Things around you that come from Japan

HISTORY
- Famous Japanese people
- Traditions

HOME ECONOMICS
- Different kinds of food
- Cooking a simple Japanese rice dish
- Eating with chopsticks

Extension Activities

Geography
- Do we eat any foods that come from Japan? Investigate packets and labels.
- What is the weather like in Japan? Look for clues in the photographs and text of this book.
- Ask the children to try to work out which photographs in the book show different types of settlement.

Maths
- Make your own Japanese money, with yen. Talk about what things you might buy if you went to Japan.
- Look at some weather data, in numerical form, for Japanese locations. Make graphs to show temperature and hours of sunshine.

RE
- Investigate the Buddhist religion.

History
- Look at photographs in this book, and search for buildings and locations that are modern. Can the children find any examples of buildings or places that they think are old-fashioned?

DT
- All children will probably have something in their home that was made in Japan. Ask them to investigate and see what the class as a whole can come up with.

Glossary

Chopsticks A thin pair of sticks that Japanese people use to pick up their food.

Dormant A name given to volcanoes that have not erupted for a while.

Earthquakes When the ground shakes violently, caused by great pressure inside the Earth. They often cause a lot of damage.

Judo A form of wrestling.

Karate A traditional way of protecting yourself using only your hands and feet.

Kimono A loose-fitting, wide-sleeved robe. It is tied with a sash.

Martial arts Sports that use ancient ways of fighting and protecting yourself, without weapons.

Sumo wrestling An sport with competitions between huge men.

Tatami A mat made from rice straw.

Terraced land Hillsides that have had 'steps' cut into them to make flat land for farming.

Typhoons Strong winds and huge amounts of rain that often cause flooding.

Volcanoes Mountains with craters from which hot rocks, ash and steam are thrown out.

Further Information

Information books

A Family from Japan by Simon Scoones (Wayland, 1997)
A Flavour of Japan by Teresa Fisher (Wayland, 1999)
Make it Work! – Japan (Two-Can, 1995)
Postcards from Japan by Zoë Dawson (Zoë Books, 1996)
Step into Japan by Fred Martin (Heinemann, 1998)
A Visit to Japan by Peter and Bonnie Coop (Heinemann, 1998)

Fiction

Turtle Bay by Saviour Pirotta (Frances Lincoln, 1997)

Useful Addresses

Japan National Tourist Organization, 20 Savile Row, London SW1X 1AE.
Tel: 0171 734 9368, Fax: 0171 734 4290

Index

All the numbers in **bold** refer to photographs